Will Taylor

CAPE TOWN
MARCH 2023.

For Christopher

Happy birthday in Africa!!

I hope this book comes in handy
and serves to bring back
memories of your first trip to
this special place for years to come!

best wishes

Will.

SAFARI
SECRETS

The Big Five

Hinde & Taylor

HPH Publishing

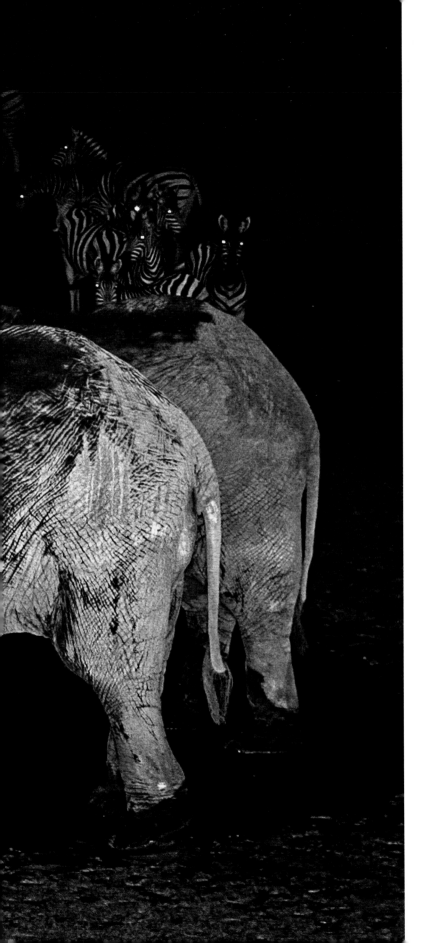

Contents

Introduction

Every single human being on the face of this planet is hard-wired somewhere way down in their genetic soul to be a tracker. As a species, the desire – even the need – to follow a series of clues and arrive at an answer or ending is deeply interesting and stimulating to us. This is what makes investigative journalism, forensic investigations, detective stories, and a whole slew of other genres of storytelling so fascinating: it is because they are connected to our primal instinct to track and find prey to survive.

It is our belief that this is also what makes any trip to the bush so exciting and rewarding. It is the anticipation of finding what you seek, coupled with the pure joy of spending time in nature, and the stories that unfold once you have found what you are looking for, that speaks to our inner being. Add a veneer of civilisation, plus human inventions allowing us to capture a precise moment of time in a photograph, which transports the viewer to that instant, and you might get the perfect blend of art and technology so many of us strive to achieve.

Gerald and I have discussed this around many a campfire, and have been asked so many questions by so many friends and clients who were companions on trips into the wild. How do you get those shots? How do you find those particular animals? How do you know what they are going to do? How? These questions, along with 'what', 'why' and 'where' formed the genesis of this book.

Over the years, we have been fortunate enough to spend tens of thousands of hours in wild places searching for the animals we were working on, trying to get the perfect photographic record of each encounter. We have worked with some of the best trackers on the continent and learnt things we could never have dreamed of – little tricks and secrets so obvious in retrospect, but hidden unless someone shows or tells you. We spent many more hours in the company of great cats waiting patiently for those brief moments of action that define their existence: hunting, mating, raising young. We waited for days on the banks of rivers to capture the perfect light, at the perfect time of year, as great herds of elephant and buffalo arrived to drink. We walked and tracked and searched thick bush for the elusive black rhino, with our hearts pounding and our nerves jangling as the signs grew fresher, and feeling so alive and privileged.

Unbeknownst to us while we were applying our respective crafts of tracking and photographing, we were building up a reservoir of knowledge and unlocking those secrets of how best to achieve our goals. Of course, this hard work came with a great deal of enjoyment too, and our appreciation and recognition of how fortunate we were to experience this prompted us to consider sharing not only the results, but the methods we had learnt.

We hope this book conveys both the excitement and exhilaration of finding and photographing Africa's great animals, and shares some of the craft and knowledge we have built up over the years, both from the tracker seat and behind the camera. Our wish was for it to be a visually stimulating work, as well as a source of information and instruction to complement any safari into the African wilderness. With this in mind, we hope the book brings you hours of enjoyment and lets you into a few secrets that enhance your next trip to the bush and the images you bring back, both in your mind and your camera.

Gerald Hinde and Will Taylor

The Photographer & the Ranger

Gerald Hinde
The man behind the camera

In 1989 the sale of Gerald's family motor business gave him the opportunity to pursue his dream of becoming a full-time professional photographer. He had been photographing wildlife since an early age, and produced and self-published his first book *The Original Gamedrive* in the last year of his business career. In 1990 he was fortunate enough to have the opportunity to spend seven months at MalaMala Game Reserve to pursue his lifelong passion for leopards, and produce his second book *Leopard*. This launched a career that led to producing 12 books and four wildlife documentaries that have all served to fulfill his mission of promoting conservation in southern Africa.

The months at MalaMala Game Reserve were also the beginning of an association and friendship with Will Taylor that has lasted more than 30 years and led to many highly successful books and television documentaries made together. *Africa's Big Five*, a book published in 1999, was one of Gerald and Will's ventures together. The book has been hugely successful and is still in print some 22 years later. The photograph of the lioness stalking on the cover won Gerald *The Wildlife Photographer of the Year* in 2000, one of many awards he has received.

For 30 years he has travelled through most of the wildlife areas in southern Africa documenting and photographing the spectacular diversity that is on offer. His photographs have been the subject of magazines and other publications, including calendars, postcards and promotional material. His deep love of the environment during a professional photographic career of more than three decades has resulted in innumerable unforgettable images. These in turn have been instrumental in winning support for wildlife conservation, one of his major goals.

Having spent years in the bush he has honed his skills in photography and as technology improved, he has stayed in touch with the latest developments. The early years served as a good grounding in the basic skills in photography so he could capture the moment in the bush. At that time there were only a handful of specialist wildlife photographers and it was difficult to get a good photograph of wild animals owing to the relatively slow lenses and low sensitivity of photographic equipment. Film had a specified ISO (referred to mostly as ASA back then) and he used ISO 50

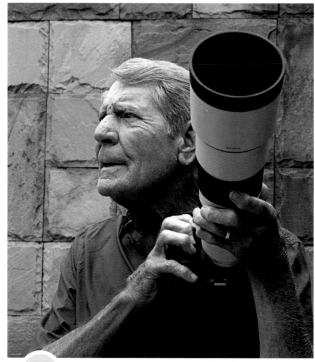

Photo secrets

Gerald Hinde loves capturing the Big Five in the frame of his camera. This sometimes has unique challenges. Here he shares some of his secrets to get that perfect shot while making the most of the bush adventure. ▲

or ISO 100 to get the highest quality image. This made capturing action shots extremely difficult in low light, and the mastering of techniques was essential to the trade. The strict rules learnt in the beginning have helped him to be more creative with the advanced cameras and lenses today.

In the pages of this book he reveals some of his photographic techniques in the hope that your experiences in the bush will become more rewarding and the images you take home will be ones you will be proud of.

Will Taylor
Always on track

Will had his first game drive at the age of three days, while being taken home from the hospital in Bulawayo, Zimbabwe to the ranch where his parents lived, in a plastic baby bath, strapped into the back seat of a Land Rover, between two bull terriers. This experience, and the years growing up in the bush, seem to have set him up for a life of adventure, with wilderness and animals predominant in everything he became involved in. Holidays while growing up in Zimbabwe were spent exploring, fishing, collecting snakes and various wild animals and birds, and generally enjoying the freedom the bush provided. This passion was transferred to his studies when he enrolled at the University of Natal, Pietermaritzburg, to study Zoology. After being awarded a Beit Fellowship and completing his master's degree, he joined MalaMala Game Reserve, where he became a senior ranger and worked closely with various conservation authorities for the next five years. Throughout his childhood and early adulthood, he was fascinated by the art of tracking, and worked with trackers in different areas and habitats to learn their tricks and secrets. When he and Gerald teamed up to do their first books and documentaries together, it seemed natural to combine their talents and the adventure continued.

Twenty-five years ago, Will founded his own specialised safari company, Khashana Travel and now, even after many years as a game ranger, film-maker and documentarian, conservationist and traveller, he still, more than anything, enjoys sharing his knowledge of the bush on safari with friends and clients. He and Gerald have produced five books together and over 20 hour-long wildlife documentaries that have been broadcast worldwide and garnered many awards. Will's deep love of the bush and his passionate support for conservation throughout the continent, along with his involvement with tourism and travel, keep him involved in the issues concerning the people and wildlife of Africa.

Ranger secrets

Having spent years guiding in the bush, Will Taylor provides tips to finding the Big Five, from tracks in the sand to looking at the behaviours of other species as indicators. These should give you the competitive advantage in the game of hide-and-seek. ◀

Good beginnings

If you're going on a safari you don't want to miss out on key photographic opportunities. A good guide will go a long way to providing local knowledge and positioning the game-viewing vehicle. Knowing where to find the animals and predicting their movements improves the chances of getting that special photo. The photographic boxes should also go a long way to you achieving that.

Chapter 1

TRACKING
SECRETS

Tracking Secrets
Finding the Big Five

In the bush, nothing is more exciting than setting off on a game drive in the fresh pre-dawn hours. There is no telling what excitement lies ahead or what drama can unfold before you, as it so often does.

The first few hours of the day are like a fresh page upon which the stories of the day are to be printed, just like the signs of what has already passed or transpired are written on the sands of the trails in wild places. Tracking is an exhilarating experience that releases feelings in us that go back deep into our distant genetic memory. The desire to follow, and the excitement of analysing and interpreting a set of clues and hints that culminates in finding exactly what you were seeking, is almost irresistible.

Whether you are on your own adventure, or being guided by a professional on safari, there are hints and clues that can help you in your quest for the Big Five. It is not just about following a set of tracks (although that is

a very good place to start, and to help we have supplied both diagrams and photographs of the tracks of each species). It is about employing all the senses, and learning a few 'tricks of the trade' from experienced trackers that can greatly increase your chances of success in tracking down even the elusive leopard.

Lions and leopard are often active at night, especially in the hot summer months, and may remain active during the crossover periods of early dawn and evening. Look for tracks along paths and roads. Because of the soft pads on their paws, which contribute to their stealth, these animals prefer to walk on sandy trails. As with most cats they are not fond of water, so at times of the year when the grass is long and wet from rain or dew, they tend to do their longer-distance moving on broad trails like roads. Once you have found tracks, ascertain how old they are. Crisp well-formed tracks in dust generally indicate freshness. If the edges have been blurred by wind, if there are other tracks of insects or birds over the cat tracks, or if the tracks are in wet sand or mud and have hardened, this indicates a slightly older clue. Establish direction of the spoor and

Catwalk

The signs that most distinguish leopard (left) and lion (right) tracks from hyena and wild dogs is that lions and leopards have large main pads with retractable claws and three lobes at the back and hyena and wild dogs have two lobes with claw marks. Leopard tracks are similar to those of lions and once the tracks have been identified as belonging to a cat, the simplest way to tell the difference is by size, with lion tracks obviously the larger of the two. ▲

follow. If you come across scat or droppings, your sense of smell and touch can let you know how close you are. Cats scent-mark bushes, so you will smell that distinctive musky smell if the animal has passed by in the last couple of hours.

Once you are on fresh tracks, it is very useful to keep stopping and listening, because now some of the best clues are auditory. Many animals give alarm calls when they see a predator, not only to warn each other and other animals, but also to let the hunter know that it has been seen and to spoil the element of surprise. In the broken woodland or bushveld of the Kruger area and southern Africa in general, some of the best sentries are **baboons and monkeys**.

Scent mark

If you are lucky enough to locate a leopard that is on territorial patrol, you will be presented with many great observational and photographic opportunities. Both males and females will turn and spray on low bushes or trees, and then rub their scent glands, which are located in their cheeks, on the bush. If marking a tree they may stretch up on their hind legs, and claw and scratch at the bark. If you are tracking a leopard, the freshness of scent marks can be easily gauged by the strength of the lingering odour of the mark; leopard urine and scent marks smell remarkably like fresh popcorn. Females are a lot more active than males when patrolling and will often get up on higher ground and move quickly through their territory giving the photographer all kinds of angles and poses. These markers warn other leopards that may be trespassing the territory is occupied and will be actively defended. ◄

Drag marks

Drag marks are an excellent clue to finding a leopard. When moving prey to be cached, the leopard will leave the signs of the broad track of the carcass with pugmarks on each side, and this will almost always lead to the discovery of a kill, and ultimately a leopard. Don't be fooled by the similar track left by the dragging lip of a white rhino or the trunk of an elephant. ►

The best angle

Look for the best angle with clean backgrounds and dramatic effects such as this large impala male with impressive horns photographed from the front to illustrate the size of the impala and strength of the leopard. The camera at low level also added a dramatic effect. ▼

![binoculars icon] **Directional gaze**

Giraffe are great allies of the tracker closing in on his quarry. Because of their height they pick up movement before other animals and stand still, transfixed on the danger. Other species of antelope such as impala will do this too, keeping their enemy in sight and making alarm calls all the while. ◄

Listen for **vervet monkeys** with their rapid 'cow-cow-cow' interspersed with excited chittering calls. Look for the monkeys in high branches of trees and observe where they are looking. **Baboons** give a more pronounced loud, sharp bark followed by an inhale, and the whole troop will start yelling at various pitches when they have a lion or leopard in sight. **Impala** are also the tracker's allies. Their alarm call sounds like a sharp loud sneeze. Again, try and find the herd and go to where they are looking. If they can see the cat, they will follow at a safe distance, calling all the while.

In thicker riverine bush and reeds in sandy riverbeds where it would normally be impossible to find a leopard with your eyes alone, kudu and bushbuck are a great help. The **kudu** has a deep explosive bellow that is unmistakable. The **bushbuck**'s bark is a little higher-pitched and not as loud. If you hear either of these animals making these sounds, it is a dead cert that they have a predator in sight.

Other subtle clues are obtained by simply observing behaviour of prey animals and noticing if they are acting out of the ordinary. A group of **giraffe** standing stock-still all looking in the same direction is a sure giveaway, as with other prey species like **wildebeest** and **zebra**.

Leopards in trees

It is a common misconception that leopards spend a lot of time in trees. They spend only a relatively small proportion of their lives aloft, but when they do they are at their easiest to find, so it is always worth scanning trees as you move along for something that looks slightly different – a dark object on a branch or a tail or paw hanging down. Leopards use termite mounds to rest during the day and as a vantage point when hunting so it is worthwhile to keep an eye on them, too. ◄

Smaller creatures that give more subtle clues with which inexperienced trackers may not be familiar are tree squirrels and the various species of francolin and spurfowl. **Tree squirrels** chatter and wave their bushy tails like flags, staring in the direction of the offender. The **gamebirds** are mostly ground dwellers and have specific alarm calls, which, if given from a perch on a bush or tree, are a sure sign of trouble. The only problem with these smaller creatures' indications are that they will be equally vociferous upon seeing a snake or bird of prey!

It is worth brushing up on the alarm calls of all the species mentioned so that you can recognise them in the bush on your next trip.

There are a lot of birds and mammals that survive by following predators, and these are worthy of mention. **Vultures** are obvious candidates here, and are great indicators of the presence of lions in particular. If you happen across large numbers of vultures perched in trees in a small area, the chances are something is up. Look to see if their crops are full (there will be a large lump where the neck meets the body) and if they are, it is likely the action is over and the lions have left the kill. If they are not, proceed to search the area. When you see vultures in the sky from a distance, try to see whether they are descending and landing, or perhaps rising on a thermal and ascending into the sky. Vultures going downwards is a good sign.

In the Kruger area, a great clue-provider is the **bateleur eagle**. This beautiful raptor is often the first to arrive at carrion, and is a good indicator of leopard activity, as they will sit in trees nearby where a kill is cached which vultures may have overlooked. Tawny eagles are worth watching for as well.

The undertakers

The image of vultures in trees is an iconic one on the African savanna. Because their preference is for dead trees, these mixed species gatherings can sometimes be seen from a long distance and can get you into the general area of a predator very quickly. ▲

Tracking the other three members of the Big Five is slightly different from the search for the cats. Although these are large, obvious animals, they can be surprisingly difficult to find. As ever, the best clues are tracks and droppings. When looking for **elephants** it will be pretty obvious if they have passed by recently. Whether elephants are travelling alone or in herds, their **footprints** are unmistakable, and the freshness of the **droppings** can be ascertained by the amount of moisture and the heat they contain. The droppings are largely recycled vegetation so get your hands dirty, break them open and feel if they still retain some body warmth. If they are still warm (depending on the time of year), it is probably within 30 minutes of when the animal passed. Fresh dung also attracts various species of butterflies, dung beetles and birds, such as yellow-billed and red-billed hornbills.

Again, stopping and **listening** is a good tactic when you feel you are closing in. Elephants are very vocal animals and quite noisy feeders, so the familiar growling and rumbling of individuals communicating, and the snap and rustle of tree branches will help you pinpoint their location.

Colour and contrast

Intentionally create fine-art photos for pictures that everyone will love. Composition is the first step towards taking images that are soothing and not jarring. Tonal and colour contrast are key elements in nature photography. High contrast images have the ability to make the subject pop out. ▶

Cooling off

On hot days when in search of large-bodied animals like buffalo or rhino, it is rewarding to start at known 'pans' or pools of water where the cool muddy water brings relief, not only from the heat and the sun, but from swarms of biting insects.

Buffalo do not require a lot of tracking and you quite often will just happen to come across them, but at certain times of year they can be difficult to find. Buffalo are water-dependent and in the dry season in areas like the Greater Kruger, herds will come down to drink at least once a day. Patrolling rivers or waterholes may yield results. In the wet season when water is freely available away from permanent sources, you can find groups of old bulls or 'dagga boys', wallowing in mud pans to escape the heat and biting insects. On bigger open plains systems like the Okavango Delta and floodplains of larger rivers, cattle egrets can be a great help. Watch for flocks of these birds flying up from the long grass.

The two species of **rhino** require different tracking techniques as they live in different areas, with some overlap in broken woodland. Both species follow well-worn trails through their territories and on the way to water sources. They mark these trails regularly and deposit their dung in middens, which are scrapes in the ground that can be quite large. Black rhino dung can be identified by the presence of sticks and twigs (bitten off at a 45-degree angle) whereas white rhino dung contains only grass. Black rhinos are frequently found in thick bush, so again, listening for movement and sitting tight can help. Oxpeckers are often present with both species and therefore listening and watching for these gregarious birds can lead you to the position of a rhino that you can't see.

Evidence of buffalo

Signs of the presence of large herds of buffalo are easily distinguishable as they are characterised by large numbers of tracks and a lot of dung. Buffalo tracks are similar in appearance to that of a domestic cow. ▲

Beat the metering problem

Capturing detail in a darker subject presents a challenge of balancing exposure, making a difference of as much as two f-stops with animals like buffalo. Shoot a test shot when arriving at a sighting and alter the light with the exposure compensation button. Get familiar with the way to make your images brighter or darker with the exposure compensation dial. Professionals are familiar with the histogram and adjust images to achieve the desired exposure. ▶

Pecking order

Oxpeckers are constant companions to rhino and buffalo.
Watching where they fly and hearing their calls can lead to the
discovery of these large beasts in reed beds and thick bush. If
you happen to be on foot, they are great alarm calls when you
are getting too close! ▲

Details

Practise a single task, looking at details and one thing at a
time when taking photos. Be fully attuned to what is going on
around you at that moment in time. Literally take in the detail
and capture the essence of the detail and photograph it. With
rhino chatty, sociable, red-billed oxpeckers tend to hang around
feeding on ticks and parasites on the rhino's hide. Watch them
and find an interesting close-up of the birds. ▶

Chapter 2

LION
SECRETS

Lion

There is not an animal on the face of our planet that holds a more important place in the human psyche than the lion. Why have they always been a symbol of majesty and power, used in human art and symbolism more than any other animal, even in places where lions have never lived?

To experience their presence in the wild will answer this question. The answer is based on a deep genetic memory born out of fear and respect for these creatures that ruled the savannas where we as a species were born.

Lion life

While it is the male lion with his majestic mane and regal bearing that is known as the king of beasts, lion life centres on the females and their relationship with each other. Their sociability, a unique facet of lion life, is what makes them perhaps the most fascinating of all the cats. The basic unit of lion social life is the pride, which consists of a group of two or more closely related females and their cubs. Each pride occupies a territory that expands and contracts over time depending on season and prey availability. A coalition of male lions, usually also related to each other, will hold sway over the territories of two or three such prides and will spend time with the pride, or will be on their own, patrolling and marking their territory and seeing off challenges from other males.

The social behaviour of lions makes them fascinating to watch when they are active. They do, however, spend a lot of their life asleep and this can be frustrating for keen photographers. Be patient and you will be rewarded.

Portraits for impact

The most important part of portrait photos is that the focus point is directly on the eye of the subject. Use low exposure values (f2.8–f4) to blur backgrounds, drawing the viewer's eye directly into the point of focus. Think of it as a conversation where a good social skill is to focus on the eyes of the person you're talking to. ▼

Courtship and mating

The circle of lion life begins and ends with courtship and mating. The measure of success in the natural world is the continuation of your genes into the next generation, and perhaps nowhere else in nature is this as savagely and physically portrayed as in the pairing of a lion couple.

When a female comes into oestrus, she immediately attracts the attention of one of the dominant males in the area. Courtship and mating can last up to four days, during which time the consort couple separate from the pride and will not eat or move far. Copulation takes place at 10 to 15-minute intervals at the peak of mating, trailing off in frequency on the last day. When mating occurs, it is a fast and furious process starting with the male mounting the female with much growling and snarling until he dismounts abruptly with the female snarling and swiping at him as he does so. The violence of these encounters is because of the great conflict going on between two highly aggressive members of a species. They are torn between the need to be social in order to survive, and the deep instincts of all cats to be solitary. It does make for wonderful photographic opportunities though, so if you come across a male and female lion lying under a tree on their own, stop and wait, and get the cameras ready.

Courting

A consort couple will have split away from the pride and may spend three or four days together. When tracking them, spend a lot of time listening as mating is quite noisy and will give you a clue as to their whereabouts. At the height of their cycle the frequency of mating may be every 10 to 15 minutes. The female usually initiates the interaction so be ready when she gets up and moves towards the male.

Flash

Dusk and dawn are the ideal times to use a flash during the day but don't hesitate to use it at other times to bring out rich colours, detail in dark areas and create dark backgrounds that make the subject pop.

Starting life in the pride

Lion cubs are born after a gestation period of only 110 days or so. They are tiny and helpless and well hidden by the female. This short gestation period allows for the female to still hunt and feed while pregnant, and for the first month after their birth, she will leave the cubs periodically to return to the pride. By two weeks, the cubs are moving around on unsteady but sturdy legs, exploring the immediate surrounds of their den, but staying still and quiet when their mother is away so as not to attract the attention of predators and scavengers such as leopards and hyenas.

The cubs are introduced to the pride at around five weeks. Quite often females within the pride will have come into oestrus at the same time and there can be two or three sets of cubs in the pride within a few months of each other in age. This helps with the sharing of suckling and baby-sitting activities, which in turn increases the chances of the cubs' survival. As it is, survival of lion cubs is very tenuous because of all the dangers to such vulnerable youngsters, as well as the conflicting urges in lion life. If there is not enough food to go around, cubs will not be protected or allowed to feed at the expense of the adults. From a selection point of view, it is more important for the mother to survive and breed again should times become tough. This fine balance between survival and death prevails in one form or another throughout the youngsters' first year and a half. From being vulnerable to predators at the den; being injured on introduction to the pride or while feeding; getting lost during hunts; not having an opportunity to get food at kills; or being born at a time when conditions or social issues within the pride are not optimum, there are numerous threats and dangers.

If new males take over the territory they will chase off older cubs and kill younger ones so the females will become reproductively receptive sooner and allow the new males to bring their own genes into the pride.

Play time

All animal youngsters are rewarding subjects to photograph but lion cubs provide special encounters. Early morning and late afternoon are typically the times when cubs are most active. Be ready to capture images of them playing, stalking everything that moves, jumping on the adult pride members or cuddling up to their mothers. The relationship between a lioness and her cubs is a special one so be ready for a tender look here or a snarl there.

Capture the moment

Shutter speeds are important for freezing movement. Increase exposure and/or ISO when using aperture priority or alternatively set the camera on shutter priority. Shutter priority allows the user to adjust the shutter speed and the camera sets the aperture. Shutter priority mode is typically denoted by Tv or S on the dial. Aperture priority mode is typically denoted by A or Av on the dial. ◂

Growing up and moving out

Those youngsters that survive to the point where they can become independent, or become part of the pride have very different destinies, depending on their sex. Young females tend to join their natal pride and grow up to become functioning members of the pride, with some migration occurring between prides. We have seen a few instances of females choosing to go off on their own, and even raise cubs on their own with no allegiance to any specific pride. Young males face a much more uncertain future. As they get close to adulthood at around two-and-a-half to three years, they are perceived as a threat to the dominant males of the pride and chased out. Frequently, small groups of brothers or half-brothers are ejected at the same time and they wander around as nomads for a while, avoiding territorial males and hunting and fending for themselves in marginal areas away from core pride territories. When they become big and strong enough to threaten other males and vie for territory, they start testing dominant males and eventually this leads to confrontation. These battles can be just a lot of noise and territorial marking, or they can progress into extremely violent and fatal interactions.

Lion speak – communication

Because of their social nature, communication is key to lion life and this is well worth watching for when observing lions in the wild. Ironically, lion communication largely revolves around trying to avoid conflict. These are animals with fearsome weapons that can do great damage to each other so reduction of aggression in their interactions is key. While observing lions and their apparent affection for each other, it is easy to believe theirs is a loving and close family set-up; and for some female pride members this may be true and the bonds are strong but they must be constantly maintained. The felids as a group have the most complicated repertoire of facial expressions of all the carnivores, and lions, being the most social felids, are at the pinnacle of this system.

All the body parts that a lion uses in interspecific visual communication – in other words when lions are talking to each other – are highlighted in black.

Black signals

Look at a lion and you will first be struck by the uniformity of the colour of the body. Now look carefully and you will see that every part of the body that is used in communication is black, as if underlined for emphasis. The lips, the nose, the rims of the eyes, the backs of the ears and the tail tassel are all in vivid contrast to the tawniness of the body. ▶

Sleepy

Lions spend as much as 20 hours a day either resting or sleeping and the best time to photograph them is early morning or late afternoon. The waking-up routine in the late afternoon before the hunt is the perfect time for photography as they yawn, stretch and interact with each other. ▼

Head rubbing

Rubbing heads is a bonding characteristic in lion prides so keep the camera ready when lions approach each other, particularly when they are lazing around or when cubs interact with adults. ▸

The mane itself is a passive form of visual communication, sending signals to intruders. A lion will bristle its mane in interactions to give an impression of bigger size. The mane also has other functions such as protection during fighting.

These visual signals are the lion's form of close-quarters communication, but they also have a whole system of long-distance communication: olfactory clues such as scent marking, and vocalisations such as roaring, to help avoid surprise meetings. When meetings do occur, or in everyday life, the aforementioned black-highlighted body parts are used in combination to convey different messages: they draw their lips back from their teeth, slit their eyes, turn their ears backwards, lash their tails and so on.

Tactile communication is most often used in bonding situations, and is extremely important and ritualised. The most frequently observed of these is the head rub. Head rubbing functions mainly as a greeting, but it is also used as a precursor to other activities such as hunting, or as a calming and 'making-up' gesture after aggression. The intensity of rubbing is a clue as to who are the most closely bonded members of a pride. Cubs invariably greet by rubbing the top of their head against the chin of an adult and then arch their whole body and tail against the adult while pressing against the chest. Full body rubs and collapsing on top of each other are common among closely bonded females.

Hunting and feeding

In the cooler months of the year, lions are more active in daylight hours, and sitting with a pride even in the warmer part of the day can be rewarding, with all kinds of interaction between the members of the pride. In the heat of summer they tend to stay in deep shade for most of the day and become active only towards dusk. Of course, the ultimate thrill while watching lions is observing them hunt and regardless of the time of day or season, there is generally a pattern of behaviour leading up to this.

There are static opportunities to watch hunts take place, and these are usually at watering points where animals gather in the dry season. There are numerous waterholes in the Kruger and other national parks throughout South Africa where lion prides display their particular life skills in the heart of the dry season, and it is worth settling down and waiting at these spots to capture the action.

In most parts of their domain, lions hunt the prey that is most readily available to them. In the Lowveld of South Africa, impala are by far the most abundant antelope

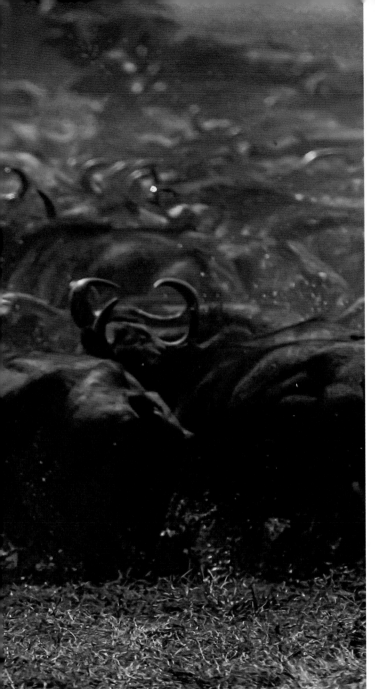

and therefore the most common item on the lions' menu. Certain prides develop the skill set to hunt giraffe and other bigger prey, with kudu, zebra and wildebeest always on the menu if the opportunity arises.

Lion-hunting behaviour is based on risk and reward; hunting big powerful animals like elephant, hippo and buffalo is extremely dangerous, but if successful, results in a huge bonanza of food with no further expenditure of energy on hunting required for a while. Lions engaging in this behaviour often raise young that are supersized and

Hunting – what to watch for

One of the females will get up, stretch and yawn multiple times, and walk over to other members of the pride to rub heads or lie down again in close contact, sometimes on top of the other cat! This will get others up and they will start moving, but lie down a couple more times before getting going. They will often lie or sit together facing the breeze to pick up scents and sounds. After a few minutes of this, they will begin to move more purposefully in a set direction, and this is the beginning of the hunt. ▲

Rare moments on camera

Capturing rare or fleeting moments can be tricky. The best advice is to be alert and ready. Make sure the camera is switched on and ready to shoot at the touch of the button before the action is over. Aperture priority with aperture set at widest (f2.8–f4) and high ISO (640 or higher) is the ideal setting.

Opportunism

Lions are highly opportunistic and will take advantage of almost any situation. In some areas, prides have even adapted to hunting highly stressed elephant populations during times of drought and will target young and sub-adult individuals. Be ready for anything.

these become the next generation adults with both the behavioural skills and physical tools to continue as mega-prey hunters.

The hunt itself starts with stalking into position and then a charge towards the animal targeted. Lions are spread out during the hunt, and if the charging lion is not successful, the prey can run into another member of the pride. With bigger animals, the lions will try to attack from the rear and drag the animal down. With large prey such as buffalo or giraffe, larger members of the pride sometimes jump onto the back or flanks of the animal to drag it down where a fatal bite is administered. This is usually a bite to the throat, closing off the windpipe and throttling the prey, but some individual lions have perfected a bite to the mouth and nose of larger antelope preventing the victim from breathing, which not only kills very quickly, but also stops the animal from giving off distress calls that might alert other lions or hyenas.

Depending on the size of the pride, things can get pretty messy from here. Although lions are socially co-operative when hunting, there are no rules when it comes to feeding and it is everyone for themselves. Smaller prey is devoured swiftly, but large animals provide food for days. Lions are not too fussy about the freshness of their food and will continue eating from a carcass long after it has begun decomposing, making for some rather distinctive smells if you are photographing nearby!

There are numerous other animals who live and feed alongside the king of the beasts. The most notorious of these is the spotted hyena whose relationship with lions is the subject of many tales, both fact and fiction. In some parts of Africa there is an ongoing battle between these two super predators, and hyenas are a constant presence at lion kills. There is little love lost between these two; hyenas are known to kill lion young when the cubs are

Ready for action

Lions mostly appear comatose as they lie around but they may suddenly sit or stand up to survey their surroundings. If you are lucky enough to be able to follow them hunting, it may be a chance of a lifetime to capture some memorable moments. Be prepared for action and make sure your camera settings are correct. Many wildlife photographers use aperture priority mode because it is fast and easy to set the aperture. Use low apertures (f2.8–f4) and high ISO (800 or more) to freeze the action. If you are using a zoom lens it is advisable to go a bit wider than necessary in order to capture all the action in frame.

found alone at their dens, and many an unwary hyena has been taken down when getting too close to the action at a kill. Hyenas are also excellent hunters, so the rivalry for food and hunting grounds is fierce. Jackals and vultures are other scavengers that are an almost constant presence. Lions share their habitat with the other big cats of Africa, namely leopards and cheetah, which tend to give way to the larger cats, though leopards have been known to kill lion cubs.

Where to find lions

Lions were once plentiful throughout Africa where they occurred in most habitats except for deep forest and jungle. They are predominantly creatures of the savanna and broken woodland, but there are populations that have adapted to mountainous terrain, coastal dunes and even desert. There are many factors that have led to the contraction of lion population, most of them to do with the encroachment of man and conflict between us and this magnificent species.

Today, there are many protected areas throughout Africa that have healthy lion populations, but the sad fact is that lions have undergone a catastrophic decline and are on the brink of extinction in all but the largest and best managed national parks.

Just over a century ago, there were more than 200 000 wild lions living in Africa. There are now only about 20 000; lions are extinct in 26 African countries and are absent from 95% of their historic range. Only six countries are known to each contain more than 1 000 lions. In just the last 20 years, the wild lion population of Africa has shrunk by 43%.

The largest and most stable populations of lions are found in the savanna woodland plains of eastern and southern Africa. In South Africa, the Kruger Park and surrounding areas still remains the best place to find lions, while in East Africa, the Serengeti and Mara ecosystems in Tanzania and Kenya are the best strongholds.

Setting the scene

Wider shots that include the landscape are the best way to tell a story with photographs. Use higher aperture settings (f8–f11) for better depth of field and ensure the focus is on the animal most dominant in the image. Leading lines also play an important part in drawing the viewer's eye towards the important section of the photograph.

Chapter 3
ELEPHANT
SECRETS

Elephant

Elephants are the largest animals to walk on the land, and they hold a great fascination for us. To see elephants in their natural habitat is one of the most awe-inspiring natural experiences you can have. It is not only because of their size that we find them fascinating to watch, it is also because of their unique nature.

Elephants, like humans, are long-lived animals, with a lifespan of 60–70 years and as such, have time to learn and accumulate experience and knowledge. Like us they have a long childhood, during which they learn about their society and their surroundings. They have tantrums when they are weaned, are naughty and are disciplined as they test the bounds of their society, go through puberty and become rebellious teenagers, form new relationships but still maintain close family ties, and then become aged and die in much the same way as we do. They show evidence of an awareness of their own mortality, and displays of true emotion indicate the presence of conscience and conscious thought. Next time you are watching a herd of elephants at a waterhole, or browsing their way slowly through the bush, consider how closely the subtleties of their behaviour match our own.

Human affinity

We have an affinity with elephants like no other animal. They are wonderfully photogenic animals and are always up to some antics. One of the first photos that we all take is a full-frame shot, which is fine (for the record), however, it's a good idea to wait until they do something with their trunks, or some other interesting activity before pressing the shutter.

Elephant life

Elephant society is divided into two separate systems existing alongside each other: male society and female society. The stable and basic unit of elephant society is the mature cow, affectionately (and scientifically) known as the matriarch, her female offspring and some close relatives. These groups can be as small as two to six or as large as 20–30 in more established family groups with older matriarchs. These smaller family groups have connections to bigger kinship groups, the next level of elephant society, and then on to more distantly related clans. These clans occupy the same home range and all the animals within that range, including the bulls, make up a sub-population. There is no doubt individuals among these smaller groups recognise and remember individuals within other groups. Occasionally we have seen gatherings of large numbers of elephants within a population when these groups come together, usually at water sources during the dry season, and I like to think that maybe long-lost sisters or cousins find each other and spend time together before parting again.

During these gatherings there is much squealing and bellowing, growling and trumpeting, but very little aggression. Elephants have elaborate greeting rituals with the placing of the tip of the trunk in each other's mouths to 'smell' who they are talking to being the most common.

The cutest one

Baby elephants are full of fun and a joy to photograph. If you come across a herd of elephants with youngsters, stay with them and it is most likely you will take home memorable photos. Keep the sunlight directly on the subject because detail in the shadows is hard to recover. However, the downside to trying to photograph baby elephants is that they tend to be surrounded by the herd and protected by their mothers.

Family dynamics

Baby elephants are the heart of the herd and live an extremely protected, enjoyable life. Their mothers and aunts are constantly on the lookout as they play and explore, but are quick to discipline the young ones if they misbehave. Growing up involves a lot of mimicking of adults, which can be entertaining to observe, and learning to use the trunk is a constant source of frustration (to the little ones) and amusement for the spectator. Keep an eye on the youngsters as they are always up to something, especially when the herd is drinking.

With elephants that spend most of their time together, greeting is more subtle, with brief body contact and trunk-to-body touches acting as communication and reassurance. Next time you have the privilege of observing elephants, notice how individuals group together and touch each other, and you will go away with a vivid picture of mothers, aunts, cousins, fathers and even the odd irritating uncle.

👀 Munching along

Elephant activity mostly involves eating and drinking, with adults having to eat upwards of 150–200 kilograms of food a day. They are uniquely equipped to eat just about anything they come across. They can eat leaves, bark, pods, seeds and entire branches of trees up to six metres high. They can dig up roots, tubers, eat aquatic plants under the water and take in fruits, flowers, sedges and herbs. They can push over trees to eat roots that store highly nutritious carbohydrates in the non-growing season, shake trees to dislodge pods and seeds, wrap their trunk around large swathes of freshly grown grass in the rainy season, using their feet and toenails to help harvest this fresh bounty, or delicately pick up small fallen fruit like marulas one by one with their sensitive trunks. In fact, they can utilise about 95% of all the plants they come across. Their environment is like a giant salad bowl to them. ▲

Water

Elephants *love* water. They drink over 100 litres a day and thoroughly enjoy being in and around it. With their huge body mass, temperature control is critical, and water plays a large part in this. At muddy waterholes, they spray and slap mud on themselves, kicking and churning the mud with their feet into a good sticky consistency. An elephant uses its trunk to throw mud and water onto the back of its massive ears which they then flap to transport cooler blood from the rich vein network in the ears to the core of the body. When well plastered in mud, they emerge from their bath and throw sand and dust on themselves and conclude their ablutions by rubbing and scraping against trees and rocks. All this activity not only cools them down, but helps control parasites and biting flies that live on their craggy skin, and also contributes in no small way to the social bonding and well-being of herds.

In bigger bodies of water such as dams and rivers, elephants love to immerse themselves, and swim and play.

From a photographer's (or just a casual observer's) point of view, this is the very best setting in which to spend time with these amazing animals, so station yourselves at water sources whenever you can.

Elephant bulls

The structure of male elephant society is somewhat simpler although still highly social. Only old bulls, or bulls in a condition known as 'musth' spend any length of time on their own. Bulls usually occupy bachelor ranges away from the areas with family groups, often spending time along permanent rivers, while family groups tend to come down to the river just to drink and then leave almost immediately. Older heavily tusked bulls are occasionally escorted by two or three younger bulls who are more alert and aggressive than the old fellow, and warn him of the presence of danger. The old hunters used to refer to these youngsters as 'askaris', the Swahili word for policeman.

Reproduction and musth

Male elephants, of course, are driven by the motivation to reproduce and pass their genes on to future generations, and nature has designed an interesting system for this purpose. Elephant bulls have a hormonal switch that brings them into a state of reproductive readiness called 'musth', a word that tongue-ties rangers and hunters in Africa. This Urdu word is used by the Mahouts in India who have spent centuries working with elephants, and are deeply knowledgeable about their behaviour. Bulls start coming into musth at around 20 years of age and spend about four to six months a year in musth. A musth bull is recognisable by secreting temporal glands behind his eyes, a dribbling penis sheath that stains the insides of the back legs, a strong musky odour and a bad temper. While in this condition, bulls wander away from their range and cover huge distances to find receptive females in family groups. Non-musth bulls and herds with no receptive females stay well away from these aggressive interlopers but other musth bulls may engage them in sometimes terrible conflicts over mating rights. This wandering may help to promote genetic diversity in sub-populations of elephant, and indeed it seems cows are more receptive to a strange bull in their range than the local males they are more familiar with.

What to watch for

As this is essentially a field guide that we hope will provide aid when observing and learning about the Big Five, it would be helpful to point out some key elements of elephant behaviour that might be useful. Where to see them and what to look for have already been covered, but because of their huge size and strength, it is worth knowing how to be safe around wild elephants, or more precisely how to stay out of trouble.

To begin with, it's essential to find out what the situation and conditions of a specific elephant population are. Elephants throughout Africa are under different pressures and exhibit a wide range of behaviour around humans. In areas where there are negative interactions with humans, such as hunting, poaching, being trapped or poisoned by local farmers when crop raiding, or in areas where they are hiding out from human encroachment because of all these stressors, elephants can be extremely dangerous. In national parks and private game reserves where they are not persecuted or disturbed by humans, they can become well habituated to the presence of vehicles, and this is the optimal way to spend time with these wonderful creatures.

The small things

Detail is what our eyes, as photographers, so easily miss and viewers are intrigued by seeing detail in a photo. Approach your photography like an architect or artist by attending to detail and capturing it as a moment in time. ▶

Staying safe around elephants

Having established how the elephants in a particular area behave, whether well or badly, it is useful to know the signs of responses you might get from an elephant. Firstly, mothers with babies are generally the most unpredictable and aggressive. Give them lots of space and let them feel comfortable; never box them in or block an escape path if you can help it. Bulls in musth are the next most aggressive and should be treated with great respect.

There are phases of threatening behaviour that an elephant goes through before charging.

Generally the first few levels are just to shoo a threat away. Standing tall and making themselves look bigger with ears flared out is an early-stage posture of a nervous or aroused elephant. Head-shaking so that the ears slap against the head, and the swishing forward of the trunk towards the threat, usually accompanied by a blast of air or a trumpet, is a step up. A charge may follow any of these actions, and may be preceded by the animal rocking backwards and forwards with one foreleg extended so that the foot is resting on the heel. The mock charge may vary in intensity from a few steps to a full lumbering run at the enemy, pulling up just short and blasting noise from the trunk and throat. A more serious charge involves the trunk curled up under the mouth, ears laid flat and tight against the ears, a more 'crouched' posture and, scariest of all, no noise or vocalisations.

However, elephants are unpredictable and have been known to charge and carry out a full-blown attack with no warning or provocation at all. Stay alert and always make sure you, or the elephant, has an escape route should things get risky.

Adrenaline rush

We all want to get that shot of a charging elephant but unless you are with a trained guide, it is advisable to rather move out of the way instead of standing your ground to get the photo. Over time it is possible to read elephant behaviour but they remain unpredictable. Rather stay safe and miss the shot.

Sun flare

There are basically no rules for sun flare except that it is all about creativity. Narrower apertures (f8) will be soft and diffused, and wider (f2.8–f4) will be stronger and more defined. An aperture of f5.6 and ISO of 640 with aperture set at matrix gave this photo the desired effect.

Chapter 4
LEOPARD
SECRETS

Leopard

The leopard has always been the most elusive and mysterious of the animals that make up the Big Five. Its stealth and guile are only outweighed by its supreme beauty, and it is the combination of all these qualities that make it the ultimate prize on any photographic safari.

In the past it was almost impossible to get a decent sighting of a leopard. All you might see was a flash of spots in deep undergrowth, or the glitter of eyes in a spotlight that turned into a shadow melting into the night. This state of affairs has changed and now in some parts of Africa, leopard sightings are commonplace.

Leopards can be found in virtually any habitat and the success of the species lies largely in its ability to carve a niche for itself wherever it lives. This animal is the blueprint for feline design; the ultimate cat distilled down through millions of years of evolution. Powerful, fast and silent, it can take down prey from the size of a mouse to an eland, some 5 000 times larger. These physical attributes are complemented by an uncanny mental agility and plasticity of behaviour.

Leopard life

The life of a leopard is essentially a solitary one, which tends to suggest an uncomplicated social structure but this is far from the truth. Male and female leopards are both strongly territorial and the way in which their territories are set up is fairly complex. Adult female leopards mark and defend a territory against other members of their own sex, as do males, but a male's range may contain the territories of four or more females.

The ultimate

Leopards are a wonderful sighting and it pays to be patient around them, waiting for the perfect shot. Their fur is particularly beautiful so try to take photographs that highlight the sun bouncing off it. Get the sun behind you to catch the intensity of their eyes so that you have the tightest possible focus on them.

For female leopards, the two most important resources in a territory are the availability of prey, and the number of safe den sites in which they can raise their cubs. For male leopards, of course, the determining resource is females. A male will command a range that can contain up to six adult females. Any interloper will have little chance of associating with one of the resident females for long enough to mate before the dominant male detects his presence, so exclusive mating rights go to the resident male.

Both males and females mark their territories regularly in a variety of ways. The most important and long-lasting territorial marking is done with scent. Both sexes mark in a similar fashion. They approach a marking post, usually a tree or a bush, and rub their face and head on the trunk or leaves before turning and spraying a few drops of urine onto the post. Another form of scent marking is scraping with the hind legs and urinating or defecating on the scrape.

Vocalising is the other form of territorial advertisement. The call is best described as a sound like a saw scraping across dry wood and is really a series of loud grunts spaced close together with a sharp inhalation between each grunt.

Courtship and mating

Of course, the point of all this marking of territory and vocalisation is to get the sexes together when the time is right. Mating is a noisy, violent affair with neither party seeming to enjoy the activity very much. Leopards detest being together and this courtship is seen, at best, as a necessary evil.

Birth and growth

A pregnant female will seek out a den site when she is close to giving birth after a gestation period of 100–112 days. Experienced older females will have several sites already picked out for when the time comes. Rocky outcrops and dense bushes are popular sites, and once cubs are born, their mother is very secretive in her comings and goings. Litter size is generally between one and four, with two cubs being the most common. For us humans, this makes for some highly entertaining viewing and photography as the cubs start exploring the area around the den site, and play is the order of the day when their mother is present. When she leaves to hunt, the cubs retreat into the den and stay silent until she returns. Predation on leopard cubs is high, and all sorts of dangers lurk. Apart from hyenas and other scavengers and predators, rock pythons and birds of prey are not above taking small cubs as a snack.

At some private lodges in the Sabi Sands Game Reserve in South Africa, female leopards have taken to giving birth to their cubs in the camp – often under building structures – where other predators are unlikely to venture. Over time the cubs raised in the surrounds of the camp have become completely at ease with human traffic and are seen – even as adults – walking through the camp or sleeping on outside furniture.

The instinct to hunt, and the evolvement of the techniques involved, develop with play at the den site. At first blush the games look adorable and fun, but on closer observation you can see the deadly intent behind all the playful rough and tumble. Every stalk and pounce of brother or sister is a mock ambush, and bites to the neck and head start early with 'killing' intent.

Cubs suckle for the first three months but may start taking meat at two months old. At around six months, their mother begins to show aggression towards them and this increases until they are deserted or actively chased off between 14 and 18 months. Female cubs are sometimes rejected earlier than males. Some male cubs remain close to their mother until they are two years old, frequently stealing kills as they are now larger than her. But male cubs have to avoid conflict with the territorial male and are forced to disperse from their natal territory at around two years old.

Lights, camera, action

Leopard cub sightings are few and far between so when the opportunity arises, get that camera ready to take a lot of photos. The cubs tend to be most active early mornings and early evening when the light is at its best but sometimes difficult to manage, especially if there is some action. To freeze the movement, use high ISOs (800/1600) with the lens wide open (f2.8–f4). Shutter priority or aperture priority both work well in these situations. Early mornings and late afternoons is the time that the aperture changes rapidly so watch the setting.

Cat gymnastics

Apart from being probably the most powerful of the big cats (weight for weight), leopards are also extremely agile and flexible. The feats they can get up to and the places and positions they can get their bodies into is almost unbelievable. When leopards are interacting with each other, while fighting or playing for example, stay focused and set a high shutter speed to capture the action. As they drag prey up trees or jump from branch to branch while exploring or hunting, the photographer can get great action shots. Be prepared.

Hunting and feeding

A great range of techniques and activities are employed by leopards to procure prey, from epic wrestling matches on the ground with much larger prey, to aerial capture of monkeys and birds while jumping from tree to tree. Whatever their prey, hunting normally involves a similar pattern of searching for a victim, stalking to very close range and then a pounce or a rush followed by a kill administered either by a throat bite or suffocation. Leopards use a combination of all their senses: sight, sound and smell are all important. Lions tend to rely on their hearing to detect prey, while cheetah are mostly sight hunters, but leopards rely on all their considerable powers in equal measure. They will detect their prey from some distance off and begin a single-minded stalk towards it. This is where another of the leopard's weapons is apparent: extreme patience. Once a target has been singled out, the hunter waits until the animal has moved out of range and then closes in after it, picking an area with sufficient cover to slowly narrow the gap between itself and the prey in order to attack.

Inexperienced, younger leopards are often less patient and ruin their chances by rushing in on prey before getting close enough. When conditions are right and animals are moving towards the hunter, an observer might witness the most spectacular of ambush kills. In some parts of Africa some individuals have specialised in lying in wait in flowering trees such as the sausage tree (Kigelia africana). Antelope will forage under the tree for the highly nutritious fallen flowers and get a nasty surprise when a spotted cat falls out of the tree right onto their back!

Panning

The chances of using the words leopard and aardvark together are extremely rare and one of those moments not to be missed on camera. To photograph something unique and unexpected as this make the many hours of waiting worthwhile. Fill flash helps to make the subject pop out when the light is low. Panning photography is a technique requiring a bit of practice and can create a sharp subject combined with a background that features motion blur. Use a slow shutter speed while moving the camera along to create motion blur in the background. ▲

Once an animal is captured, a fatal bite is quickly administered, the technique depending on the size of the animal. Smaller prey items are dispatched with a quick bite to the throat or back of the head, which immediately immobilises the animal. Larger victims, such as antelope or warthog, are killed by a bite to the throat, blocking the windpipe and causing suffocation. This technique also serves to prevent the animal from giving any kind of distress call that could be heard by other predators and scavengers.

With larger prey species, different leopards exhibit remarkably similar behaviour. Females in particular become noticeably agitated and nervous once they have killed and this is because an animal normally manages to get off a few distress calls before dying. In areas where lion and hyena are common, the leopard can expect unwanted company shortly after.

The cat will then grasp its prey, and straddling the carcass with its front legs, will begin to drag it from the scene of the kill.

Once in a suitable area, the leopard begins to look for a place to cache the kill, usually a tree with a long trunk. Securing its grip on the prey's neck, the leopard jumps into the tree, dragging the carcass upward with a display of immense strength. When the carcass is safely in the fork of a few branches, the leopard will rest a while before settling down to feed at leisure. Other caching behaviour includes covering the entire carcass with leaves and dirt to hide it from aerial scavengers and to cover up scent.

When looking for leopards on your own in a national park, scan trees where prey might be stashed, but also listen and look for all the clues mentioned in the tracking chapter. Alarm calls of monkeys and baboons, and the snorting or barking of antelope are a dead giveaway.

Follow the followers

Keep an eye open for hyena moving through the bush. Hyena often follow the resident leopards when they are hunting knowing full well that the moment the leopard makes a kill, they can swoop in to try and claim the victim from the leopard. If hyena are lying about, look around in the trees for any sign of a hoisted leopard kill. ◄

Get down low

Getting down low does not necessarily mean getting onto your belly (although it's a good idea when it is safe to do so) but rather eye level, which could mean the animal is on a rock or a tree. Photographing from a low angle puts the viewer into the animal's world creating an intimate view and connection with the subject.

Special effects

After you have mastered the basics, develop your creativity by experimenting. This can be done in many ways with slow shutter speeds, over- or underexposing, panning, stitching in post-production, flash sync, etc. This photograph was taken with a one-second shutter speed, f2.8, ISO 1250 with backlighting from a spotlight.

Chapter 5
RHINO
SECRETS

Rhino

The two species of rhino that occur in Africa have been at the forefront of conservation efforts on the continent since the turn of the century. They are magnificent creatures that evoke a deep response in us, and the chance to see and photograph them is enhanced by knowing we have had some success in keeping them around, particularly in southern Africa.

Finding rhinos

Because they are the rarest member of the Big Five, Gerald and I quite often found ourselves desperately tracking rhinos at the end of a safari so our guests could fulfil their goal of photographing all of the Big Five species. Both species of rhino move along well-worn paths and pick the easiest route through areas when they are on patrol or moving to and from water. They have to drink every day

(sometimes twice a day) and this makes anticipating their movements a little easier. But as many a ranger will tell you, a slight change in weather, a little winter wind or cold snap and rhinos simply disappear. White rhinos in particular spend most of their time grazing out in the open and will head for the thick stuff and wiggle their way in to places where they lie down and wait out the weather, and so cannot be found for love or money! Well-marked rhino trails frequently run along the edges of water courses, or dongas, which also happen to be excellent habitat for leopard, so it isn't uncommon to bump into one when searching for the other.

Mud, glorious mud

Thick-skinned, big-bodied animals cannot resist the lure of a muddy waterhole on a hot summer's day. The cooling effect on their skin and the chance to reduce their core temperature is just a part of it. The mud also serves as a sort of hardening body wrap that they can rub off on trees and rocks around the waterhole to remove embedded, irritating biting insects. It is like a visit to the spa. Always know the last waterholes to dry out in the area you are working in and visit regularly on hot days. ▾

Rhino bulls

Territorial marking and patrolling is a serious business for dominant bull rhinos, and following one on a patrol is a fascinating experience. A bull maintains 20–30 dung middens within his territory, with larger middens situated at boundaries and corners of his prescribed area. A midden is a scraped zone in which the bull defecates regularly while patrolling his paths. When he arrives at one, he defecates and moves backwards, kicking at the dung with slow, ritualised kicks, then moves forwards dragging his feet in a stiff-legged slow march. This behaviour may serve to mark the soles of his feet with scent and is tracked through his area as he patrols. While moving from midden to midden

the bulls also spray urine onto bushes, which is quite a sight as the spray shoots out backwards from behind their legs like a hugely powerful lawn sprinkler.

A bull will tolerate other dominant males within his territory, particularly a neighbour, as long as the visiting individual acts submissively. This arrangement is necessary because those with no water in their territory must have an easement through a neighbouring territory to waterholes or rivers to drink. If a dispute occurs, it is usually settled fairly amicably but when it escalates, fights between bull rhinos can be violent, protracted and bloody affairs. On one memorable occasion we watched a territorial stand-off between two massive white rhino bulls that lasted almost a full day. For the first couple of hours there was

Midden

Rhino middens are fascinating ecosystems. While they serve an important function to the rhinos, they also provide a nutrient-rich habitat to a huge range of animals. Insects thrive in them, with the most famous arthropod visitors being various species of dung beetles. Birds such as hornbills and drongos spend a lot of time here picking out nutritious morsels and emerging insects, while baboons and some antelope also pick through the huge piles of goodness for a snack. Middens can provide us with clues, too: a white rhino midden is filled with purely grassy remnants, while a black rhino midden contains many short sticks and twigs bitten off at a diagonal across their length, which indicates their browsing habit. ▶

some vocalising and a little fencing and pushing, while the visiting male, well outside his boundaries, continued to stand his ground. The fight quickly escalated when the larger bull suddenly dipped his head and thrust upwards into the neck and shoulder of his opponent, sinking his horn deep into his flesh. With slow, deliberate and massively powerful thrusts they gored each other for more than half an hour, until the bloodied and defeated visitor struggled back to his turf where we found him dead later that night. The badly wounded victor survived the fight, but lost his territory on the very next challenge and staggered off into obscurity.

Mark this well

Bull rhinos have a remarkable ability to spray vast quantities of urine backwards through their hind legs to mark bushes and trees as they patrol their territories. This unusual picture of a black rhino on the plains of the Maasai Mara, marking his way around a thicket, captures a great image of this normally shy and secretive creature out on the open plains. ▲

Textured for character

Photographing rhino usually takes a bit of patience if more than a portrait photo is wanted so it pays to wait around for the moment to present itself. Their thick, textured skin is very detailed and full of crevices and wrinkles adding character to the image. If there are shadows, this is a good time to use fill flash. Once again watch for those chatty, sociable, red-billed oxpeckers for added interest.

Rhino life

White rhinos are generally more socialable than black rhinos. The common grouping in both species is to see a mother and calf together, but white rhino youngsters recently rejected by their mother will tag along with another female and her new calf and maybe also her last calf, so seeing three or four white rhinos together is not unusual. In favourite sleeping places and at watering points there

can be 10 or more rhinos together – a 'crash' or 'scrum' – and is quite spectacular. As white rhinos are grazers and black rhinos are browsers, you generally find black rhinos in thick vegetation, more often than not just an individual or a female and calf. Perhaps because of the secretive environment of their feeding habitat, or their generally nervous nature, black rhinos are irritable, aggressive and fearless once engaged. I have seen the gentle side of black rhino in captivity, but there are few I have encountered in the wild that haven't been intent on doing grievous bodily or vehicular harm.

Apart from the habitat they occupy (thicker bush for black rhino, open grasslands for white), the two species are fairly easy to tell apart.

White rhinos are much bigger, bulkier animals. They are specialist grazers and their wide, square lip is an adaptation to this and one of their most distinguishing features. White rhinos also have a big ball of muscle on their back behind the head which is known as a nuchal hump (again an adaptation for lifting and lowering the head while engaging in grazing). Their backs also appear straighter and more horizontal than the black rhino's back, which has a hollowed appearance.

Black rhinos have a hooked prehensile top lip adapted to their browsing lifestyle, their head is shorter and more rounded, as are their ears.

Behaviours to look for that are different between the two species include the carriage of the head. Black rhinos' heads are held high whereas white rhinos tend to keep their heads down. There is a difference in how black and white rhinos position their calves, too. Black rhinos run with their calf behind them, and white rhinos keep their calf in front of them when moving fast.

When taking photographs, white rhino are easier to get close to, but watch for any movement of their tail. If you see them start to curl their tail away from their body it is a sign of irritation and they may be getting ready to run away. Back off and wait a little while and they will soon calm down.

Rhinos love water, particularly on hot, windless summer days. It is always a good idea to stake out muddy rainwater pans in known rhino territory. Some of the best photographic opportunities occur here as rhinos wallow and mud-bathe – and sometimes even sleep – in the delicious muddy mess. Quite often you will find well-polished rubbing posts near waterholes that are either stumps of hardwood trees, or sides of rough barked trees still growing in the area. Rhinos will spend a good length of time scratching and rubbing hard to get to parts of their anatomy they can't normally reach, which makes for some amusing shots.

Because they are large grey animals and generally slow-moving, Gerald has always said the best shots are taken when rhinos are doing unusual things. Anticipation of their behaviour and patience on your part will lead to better opportunities. For example, following a bull rhino on patrol, or watching a rhino come down a steep slope into a river bed, can result in rewarding images.

Rhino occupy a vitally important place in the soul of Africa, and it would be a sad day if the huge bulk of the bull rhino standing four-square on the plain with his iconic horn ceased to be. As with all the other myriad species of animals that make up the complex web of the African ecosystem, rhino are dependent on us protecting the habitats in which they thrive, and we must be diligent in keeping rhino at the forefront of our conservation efforts.

Golden light

Much of the visual art of photography is the phenomenon of good lighting. Fortunately, most safari outings take place early morning and late afternoon during the golden hours. Take advantage of these times when the animals are most active and the lighting is golden and perfect to capture stunning photos.

Chapter 6

BUFFALO
SECRETS

Buffalo

As a casual observer you would be forgiven for looking at a large herd of buffalo grazing on the African plains and wonder why such a seemingly placid bovid has been included in the Big Five. But if you were to ask a group of experienced African hunters and guides which of the Big Five is the most dangerous, a large percentage of them would place the buffalo firmly at the top of that list.

Left alone, this is a placid, if easily irritated animal that generally goes about its own business. But when roused, the Cape buffalo, particularly the bull, has a turn of speed, a reserve of strength, and a singularity of purpose that is frightening.

The social organisation of large herds of buffalo is interesting to observe. People ask, "Who leads the herd, and who starts them moving?" It has long been assumed that buffalo society is matriarchal but it is the prime reproductive bulls that are dominant in the herd. The leaders of movements however, are frequently individuals that are not dominant nor even adult. These are known as pathfinders and seem to take the lead in turns. The rest of the herd consists of subgroups, or clans, of related cows and their offspring from the last three years, each group attended by a number of sub-adult or adult males. There is a direct linear hierarchy among the cows and a set hierarchy among the bulls.

Down at the waterhole

Photographing from underground hides is an absorbing and adrenaline-filled experience. This is the opportunity to get down low and close so that you can capture images with impact. Many hides are located in Big Five territory and the possibility of photographing big animals such as elephant, buffalo and rhino is increased because they are regular visitors to the waterholes at the hides.

Buffalo bulls

It is the older males who have left the herd to form bachelor groups that have created the buffalo's reputation as a mean and fearsome adversary. These grumpy old men are called 'dagga boys' by local trackers in South Africa. Dagga is the Zulu word for mud and is a reference to the older bulls' penchant for mud-bathing to ward off biting insects and flies with which they are normally infested as they lose their hair in their old age. The mud forms a soothing, cooling coat on the skin, and when the dried mud is rubbed off on a stump or tree, it helps removes those irritating, clinging parasites.

In the hot months during and just after the rainy season, mud wallows and small bodies of water are the best places to look for groups of these bulls, and provide good photographic opportunities.

 Muddy texture

Like elephant and rhino, buffalo love mud wallows and they often lie around in the mud. They need to drink daily so you have a good chance of encountering them either on their way to or leaving water. The big herds stir up a lot of dust and this makes for good images. ◀

Photographing buffalo

There is no need to go deeply into the biology of buffalo, but there are some interesting facts about their behaviour and some good guidelines for photographing them. Gerald and I have always found that large-bodied, grey and black animals like rhino and buffalo are really difficult to get anything but portrait shots of, unless you work on light and activity, so here are some pointers.

Firstly, buffalo are dependent on water. They need to drink at least once a day and in the hot months at the end of the dry season, it is almost always twice a day. Coupled with this, they need to travel long distances away from water sources in their area to feed, as most of the grazing has been annihilated by other grazers and elephants.

This presents the casual observer and keen photographer alike with a number of opportunities.

During the hot dry months before the arrival of the rainy season in southern Africa, the sunsets are remarkable because of the amount of dust and smoke in the air, and towards evening, large herds of buffalo come down to rivers and other bodies of water to drink. This is a good place to position yourself so you are shooting into the sun as the buffalo come down to drink. You can get amazing backlit shots of buffalo in the orange dust when they break into a gallop on the way down to the water, and then there is lots of activity when they splash about.

At this time of year, they need to move large distances, and the lack of nutritious grasses causes the buffalo to weaken rapidly before the onset of the rains. This makes them particularly vulnerable to predation, and the lions in any given area know this. Lion-on-buffalo interactions increase dramatically, and this also offers incredible opportunities to get dramatic wildlife shots.

Predation on buffalo

The interaction between buffalo and lion is the pinnacle of predation on the African savanna (the heavyweight title fight, if you will) and for those who have witnessed this spectacle, it is hard to forget. For all that a herd of buffalo looks like an unorganised shambling mass, they employ innate and specific tactics when under threat. The youngsters and weaker animals crowd into the centre of the herd, and the bulls and older cows form a line of defence in front of the lions. Many a lion has come to grief on the sharp horns of a buffalo defending its herd, and lions have to be extremely skilled and patient to take on this powerful prey, even when the buffalo is in a weakened state.

The lions try to get the herd to break and run so they can pick off weaker and smaller members, while the herd does its best to move in a cohesive unit with its defensive line always facing the enemy. The action is intense and more often than not, the lions are seen off.

The big one

When lions hunt bigger prey like buffalo they rarely hide and stalk, but run in while calculating the size and vulnerability of their desired prey. Their hope is that panic will split the herd. This activity may continue for a long time as the lions pursue the buffalo. Keep your camera ready because there will be plenty to photograph. Make sure the aperture setting is wide open and the ISO rating is higher than 800. Darker animals will overexpose the image so it is advisable to compensate by adjusting the exposure compensation button to about -1 or 2. Take a test shot to determine the compensation needed.

Buffalo life

Another great time of year to be around buffalo is during the mating and calving seasons that begin with the onset of rains. It is a busy and turbulent time as bulls, flushed with hormonal vigour and filled with aggression, begin to stake their claim to the sub-units or family groups of the herds. They engage in aggressive displays such as horning vegetation or the ground, tossing soil in the air and rubbing the neck along the ground. There is a lot of chasing and movement in the herd, which occasionally breaks out into titanic battles between dominant bulls, but most conflicts are resolved by sparring where the contestants clatter and hook their horns together and

attempt to throw each other off balance. Even this more subdued form of conflict can result in severe injury, such as a broken leg that usually seals the fate of the vanquished one.

A herd that is stationary and grazing will be spread out, each of the sub-groups remaining together, and when they pause during the day to lie down, rest and ruminate, the members of the clans tend to lie together in tightly packed smaller groups. When on the move, everyone blends together in a tight bunch or long line.

Buffalo appear to have no real preference for nocturnal or diurnal activity. According to weather, forage availability, moon phase and many other factors, they are active and feed both day and night.

Buffalo talk

When on the move, there is a lot of vocal communication between individuals and this is one of the best ways to locate a buffalo herd over long distances, or in thick bush. On their way to drink there is a specific long, drawn-out 'maaaaaa' call that spreads through the herd, gaining in excitement as the leaders get closer. When at rest, or grazing, vocalisations are grunts or sharp moos that allow individuals to keep in touch or chase off strangers.

Enjoying buffalo

While it might seem that sitting with a herd of buffalo is not the most exciting option when in Big Five territory, we would encourage you to take the time to do so. There is always something going on. A large buffalo herd generates its own moving ecosystem, and apart from interaction with large predators and other members of the Big Five, there are many other smaller interactions going on. Fork-tailed drongos follow the herds, flitting from branch to branch and picking off insects disturbed by hooves in the grass, western cattle egrets walk alongside individuals and do the same, flying up and settling on the saddles of herd members to hitch a ride. Oxpeckers ride along on the massive beasts and offer the chance of great photos as they investigate ears and nostrils for the ticks and fleas they feed on.

Steer clear

Don't be fooled by the placid countenance of the ruminating buffalo. This is an animal that demands a lot of respect. Many rangers and trackers with years of experience have fallen foul of these wily beasts while tracking them on foot.

Chapter 7

THE OTHER FIVES

Buffalo weaver

The Little Five

Ant lion, tortoise, buffalo weaver,
elephant shrew and rhino beetle

An activity that is fun to do (especially when you have youngsters on safari with you) is to look for the Other Fives. The Little Five are all creatures that bear the names of their mammal counterparts. Some are easily found while others take a bit of searching. Catching an ant lion provides a lot of entertainment. They are the larvae for nocturnal flying insects that make traps to catch ants in fine sand. You need to trick them into striking at a fake ant, and then scoop them up.

Ant lion

Rhino beetle

Elephant shrew

Leopard tortoise

Lappet-faced vulture

Warthog

Spotted hyena

The Ugly Five

Spotted hyena, warthog, marabou stork, lappet-faced vulture and wildebeest

There is always much debate as to who should make it into the Ugly Five, but these are the most common choices. We happen to think warthogs are cute rather than ugly, but all of these are contenders.

Wildebeest

Marabou stork

Porcupine

The Shy Five

Bat-eared fox, mongoose, porcupine, aardvark and aardwolf

As the name suggests, these creatures are quite difficult to find, and one must be in the right place at the right time to see the nocturnal and evasive aardwolf, or the aardvark. Both of these animals are termite eaters. Although they are fairly common in some parts of Africa, they are seldom seen.

Mongoose

Aardvark

Aardwolf

Bat-eared fox

Cheetah

Caracal

Five Other Cats

Cheetah, caracal, serval, black-footed cat and African wild cat

There are five other true cats that can be found on safari and of course we are all familiar with the majestic cheetah, the fastest of all the land mammals. Serval are cats of the open plains that occur in some drier areas, but like the caracal are difficult to see unless you have help from rangers and trackers who know where to find them. African wild cats and black-footed cats are nocturnal creatures, and if you are lucky you will pick up the gleam of their eyes by spotlight on night drives.

Black-footed cat

African wild cat

Serval

Chapter 8
PHOTOGRAPHY
SECRETS

Taking Photos like a Pro

How to get the most from
Big Five photography

If you're going on safari you don't want to miss out on key photographic opportunities. Wildlife photography is the art of documenting various forms of wildlife in their natural habitat and requires some skills and fieldcraft to capture the best moments. The lessons I have learnt come from years of trial and error and the disappointment of making mistakes that resulted in losing important images.

There are three major aspects to bear in mind:
Portrait, Action, Landscape = **PAL**

(P) settings: Use a low aperture (f2.4–f4) and ISO numbers (100/200) to get out-of-focus backgrounds and minimum noise.
(A) settings: The shutter speed must be high enough (800/1000) to freeze action and can be controlled with high aperture (f8–f11) and ISO (800/1000) numbers. Auto focus on continuous high.
(L) settings: The aperture should be set to a high (f8–f11) and ISO to a low (100/320) number.

The more technical information is listed on page 142, and it would be useful to put some time into studying it, or your camera's handbook, as this would be your first step to taking quality wildlife photos.

Portrait

Action

Landscape

Getting started

Modern camera technology is exceptional and if you're starting out, the automatic mode works well as it allows you to concentrate on the basic elements of photography. The problem with this mode is that the camera has no idea of what image you have in mind, so creativity is limited, and this is when the more flexible modes come into play.

Great, action-packed moments in wildlife photography last a mere moment and you will generally miss them if you are not familiar with the camera settings.

- Automatic mode   (A) or (Auto)
- Program mode   (P)
- Aperture priority mode   (Av) or (A)
- Shutter priority mode   (Tv) or (S)
- Manual   (M)

For beginners it is difficult to move into using **manual mode** but luckily cameras have aperture and shutter priority. These are the best ways to understanding the role of aperture and shutter speed.

Many wildlife photographers use **aperture priority** and this is also a great mode for beginners. Aperture priority allows the user to set the aperture value while the camera sets the shutter speed to match it so that it will result in proper exposure. Setting the aperture manually controls depth of field and allows for faster shutter speeds in order to freeze the action. For landscape photos, a good aperture to use would be f8–f11 and for action as wide as the lens allows (f2.8–f4).

Shutter priority is a mode used less often but it is useful for action photography. A shutter speed of anything faster than 800/1000th of a second is considered ideal for freezing a fast-moving animal or bird.

Study the various shutter speeds at which you can obtain a sharp image with your camera/lens combination. It is advisable to use a beanbag, but it is inevitable that the camera will be handheld when photographing wildlife and that is when faster shutter speeds are an important factor.

A small adjustment can make a big difference, which is why it's important to zoom in to the camera's display to make sure the image is sharp. Adjusting the shutter speed makes the image brighter or darker so it means the aperture or **ISO** needs to be changed. However, Auto ISO is a feature that is common to most digital cameras. It is a camera feature that many people tend to ignore but it is most useful for exposing images correctly.

Focus modes are confusing but in reality there are only three key modes.

- One shot
- Continuous
- Manual

One shot (S) is the most frequently used but if you are keen to photograph moving subjects, Continuous (AF-C) tracks the subject as it moves through the frame.

Composition

Composition plays a major role in capturing good images and the rule of thirds helps create well-balanced, interesting shots. It is basically a composition guideline that breaks images up into thirds, both horizontally and vertically, so there are nine pieces and four guidelines. Now place the point of interest along the left or right vertical line. Although it's good to keep these rules in your mind don't be afraid to break them.

Most people concentrate on **animal portraits** and this is the obvious and practical choice but not necessarily the most artistic one. Many aspects and imperfections in the bush add to the atmosphere and make for a good image so take some wider shots. Use your imagination and create your own unique style.

Try to take wider images because they can always be cropped afterwards.

Telephoto lenses

Telephoto lenses are necessary for wildlife photography and there are plenty of aspects to consider when choosing them. Zoom lenses allow the user to achieve a variety of compositions since there is no limit to the fixed focal length. However, they do come with a varying maximum aperture when zooming in. Prime (fixed focal length) lenses are sharper than zoom lenses, but it is generally hard to see the difference. Lenses with a focal length of 400 mm or above would be suitable.

Wide-angle lenses

If you ask wildlife photographers about what they think the best lenses for wildlife photography are, the overwhelming majority would say a telephoto lens. While telephoto lenses are indeed the go-to choice, there are plenty of opportunities for excellent photos at the other end of the focal spectrum. Wide-angle lenses (I recommend a 16–35 mm) give a totally different perspective of the animals and the environment they live in. Wide-angle photography does, however, require a bit of a rethink about your approach. A good place to start is a low perspective (underground hides for instance) giving the animal a much larger look and includes a lot of the surrounding environment. Wide-angle images make for a dynamic perspective and tend to hold the viewers attention for a

longer period. It goes without saying that wide-angle lenses are necessary for photographing landscapes and the stars. Star photography is time-consuming and requires a lot of research and practise, but is totally worthwhile. It can create jaw-dropping images.

Improve your wildlife photos

Spend time with the subject because there are patterns of behaviour that are ingrained into every animal species, and getting to know these patterns will help to produce great images.

Get up early and stay out late. The most compelling images are shot during the golden hours: just after sunrise and before sunset. The shadows are long and the lighting is golden and soft. For the most part keep the sun behind you. However, back and side lighting can be effective. Using a fill flash during the day is a handy way to eliminate shadows and brighten images in dull light.

Images that **evoke emotion** and give an insight into the animal's world resonate the most with the viewer. Being at eye level produces more natural and flattering results, inviting the viewer into the animal's world. Eye level does not necessarily mean ground level as the subject could be on a tree or a rock, for example.

Before leaving camp and after every sighting, **adjust the settings on the camera**. I recommend you set the camera on Av (aperture priority) and open the aperture as wide as possible (f2.8–f4) with the ISO set at 640. With these settings your camera is ready for any action that may unexpectedly occur. Once settled at a sighting there is time to do any finer adjustment. As you drive into a sighting the animals usually react to the vehicle so a quick shot or two is a good idea, especially with sleeping predators that may just lift their heads.

Mastering the technical aspects and developing your creativity are essential. When these are combined with patience, concentration and attention to detail you'll be on your way to making the most of any perfect moment.

Finally, remember that you are in the animal's world, you **are in their home,** so observe the rules and guidelines in place to protect them and the environment.

Enjoy the moment and try to capture what your mind sees.

Summary

- Get to know your camera.
- Adjust the settings before leaving camp and after every sighting.
- Get out early and stay out late.
- Focus is not negotiable, it's vital. Review the image on the back of the camera.
- Focus on the eye of the subject.
- Be ready to capture the action.
- Get down low for more dramatic shots.
- Take some wider shots to include the environment.

Technical information

Basic settings

The three basic settings that need mastering are aperture, ISO and shutter speed, and their use is an essential part of photography.

- **Aperture (f-stop)** – refers to the opening of a lens' diaphragm through which light passes. Lower f-stops (f2.8–f4) give more light because they represent the larger apertures, while higher f-stops (f8–f11) give less exposure because they represent smaller apertures.

- **ISO** is the camera's sensitivity to light, so higher ISO values mean more sensitivity to light, which in turn allows you to freeze action. The higher the ISO, the faster the shutter speed but it also makes the sensor more sensitive

to light and will diminish image quality by introducing noise (those multi-coloured speckles in the shadows). The improvements in camera technology are such that you can shoot at higher ISOs, but I recommend between 400 and 1600 depending on the available natural lighting. Early morning and late evening low light, for example, require higher ISOs.

- **Shutter speed** is a measure of the time the shutter is open, shown in seconds or a fraction of a second. The faster the shutter speed, the easier it is to eliminate blur, freeze motion and diminish the effect of camera shake.

Focusing modes

The four primary **focusing modes** are single, continuous, automatic and manual and they give the photographer a tremendous amount of flexibility. Single point (AF-S) is the best for still subjects and continuous auto focus (AF-C) for capturing motion. Modern cameras are equipped with

advanced autofocus systems and I suggest getting to know how to use them effectively to get sharp images. Details of the various autofocus systems can be referenced from the manufacturer's specifications.

JPEG or RAW

Whether to shoot **JPEG or RAW** is a question we all have to face at some point. There are many articles that cover this topic so if you want the technical details an internet search will give you all the information you need on the subject. The pragmatic point of view is, however, that both formats are useful. Is one format superior? JPEGs are not as good as RAWs. There is a vast difference in the amount of information retained in a RAW file. However, it is not necessary to shoot RAW all the time. I'm a professional (but hey, professionals were all amateurs once) so this is

situations, JPEGs are a better option. JPEGs are processed right within the camera based on your camera settings and can be viewed and printed without processing through Lightroom, Capture One, Photoshop or some other editing tool. They also take up less space for storage on a computer and memory card. Handy, convenient and less time-consuming – yes. Better for wildlife photography – no. Wildlife shooting means constantly changing lighting, background and subject situations and nobody has the ability to shoot the perfect exposure all the time. Shooting RAW enables you to shoot quickly and to fix exposure issues in post-processing, not to mention a lot of other possible adjustments. My advice is that you take some time and study the differences. Take into account that one day you might capture the perfect shot but you need that extra file information for presentation as a print or for publishing. In addition, the image needs some adjustments. RAW or JPEG? Shoot RAW and don't have

Chapter 9

BIG FIVE
FACTS

ELEPHANT
Loxodonta africana

Unmistakable. This is the largest land mammal on the planet with a nose prolonged as a trunk with two finger-like projections at the tip. Upper incisors are elongated into tusks. Their skin is grey or brown and wrinkled with coarse bristle-like hairs sparsely distributed on their body. Their large ears are distinctive.

MALE
Weight: **4 500–6 000 kg**
Shoulder height: **3 m**
Average life span: **55–60 years**

FEMALE
Weight: **2 500–3 200 kg**
Shoulder height: **2.5 m**
Average life span: **55–60 years**
Gestation period: **22 months**

Females first conceive at 10–12 years and have a calf every 4–9 years. A newborn weighs 120 kg and stands 85 cm at shoulder. Bulls become sexually mature at 12–14 years but generally don't mate till much later in life.

In 1930 there were between 5 and 10 million elephants spread across Africa; today there are fewer than 350 000. We know this from a thorough aerial count done over three years covering 18 African countries called the Great Elephant Census. Since its results were returned in 2016, numbers have continued to drop dramatically, particularly in East Africa where in some countries poaching and corruption are out of control.

Collective noun: **Herd**

LION
Panthera leo

The largest African carnivore, unmistakable in the field. Overall tawny colour with black markings on back of ears and black-tufted tail. Adult males have a mane of long hair surrounding the face and covering the head, chest and shoulders.

MALE
Weight: **180–200 kg**
Shoulder height: **1.2 m**
Length: **280–360 cm**
Average life span: **12–13 years**

FEMALE
Weight: **120–180 kg**
Shoulder height: **90 cm**
Length: **180–230 cm**
Average life span: **14–16 years**
Gestation period: **98–115 days**

Cubs are hidden for the first six weeks before introduction to the pride. They eat their first meat at around 10 weeks but continue to suckle from their mother and other pride females until eight months. Female offspring often stay with the pride, but males are ejected around 2½–3 years of age.

Lion numbers have reduced rapidly through the continent. An estimated 500 000 lions roamed in Africa in the 1950s; by 1990 that number had been reduced to 100 000; and the latest estimates put the number closer to 20 000. Southern Africa has the most stable population and the Kruger Park area in South Africa, along with parts of Botswana, Zambia and Zimbabwe still have good populations of lion. In East Africa, Kenya and Tanzania are the best countries to find lion, but numbers are under threat, particularly in Tanzania.

Collective noun: **Pride**

LEOPARD
Panthera pardus

A stocky, powerful, spotted cat. Background colour of coat varies from grey brown to rich gold. Spots are actually groups of spots known as rosettes.

MALE
Weight: **40-90 kg**
Shoulder height: **70-80 cm**
Length: **160-295 cm**
Average life span: **12-16 years**

FEMALE
Weight: **25-55 kg**
Shoulder height: **60-70 cm**
Length: **145-220 cm**
Average life span: **14-20 years**
Gestation period: **100-112 days**

Leopards are found throughout Africa except for the extreme interiors of the large deserts. Globally they are found at latitudes as far as 50 degrees north in Russia to as far south as the Cape of Good Hope in South Africa. The most successful of the large carnivores.

Collective noun: **Leap**

RHINO
Ceratotherium simum (white rhino)
Diceros bicornis (black rhino)

Two species of rhino occur in Africa: the black and white rhinoceros.

Both species are large grey herbivores with thick grey skin, columnar stocky legs and prominent horns on the front of the face. Differences are mostly due to feeding biology and the habitat in which they live. White rhinos are predominantly grazers of the open savanna, and black rhinos are browsers that frequent thicker bush.

WHITE RHINO
Weight (males): **1 800-2 500 kg**
Weight (females): **1 800-2 000 kg**
Weight at birth: **40-60 kg**
Shoulder height: **1.5-1.8 m**
Average life span: **35-50 years**
Gestation period: **16 months**

BLACK RHINO
Weight (both sexes): **800-1 200 kg**
Weight at birth: **20-40 kg**
Shoulder height: **1.4-1.7 m**
Average life span: **30-40 years**
Gestation period: **15 months**

Collective noun: **Crash**

BUFFALO
Syncerus caffer

A massive, thick-set bovid occurring in large herds, and smaller groups in protected areas. Males have thicker horns joined by a pronounced massive 'boss' on the head.

MALE
Weight: **600-900 kg**
Shoulder height: **145-170 cm**
Average life span: **20-30 years**

FEMALE
Weight: **570-590 kg**
Shoulder height: **130-150 cm**
Average life span: **20-30 years**
Gestation period: **11.5 months**

Collective noun: **Herd**

Acknowledgements

If it wasn't for the opportunity offered to me 30 years ago by Mike Rattray to complete the work on my leopard book at MalaMala Game Reserve, I have no idea how I would have started my professional photographic career. This relationship has continued and thanks to Alison Morphet, I have been able to complete many a project using this wonderful destination. Every single member of the MalaMala team has been exceptionally helpful over the years.

More recently, I have been privileged to work in Madikwe using the facilities at The Bush House and for this I wish to express my gratitude to Gordon and Sue Morrison.

Completing projects is time-consuming and my thanks to my family for their support, and my wife Pam for patiently waiting for me at home. A big thank you to my son Wayne who – after my neck operation in 2018 – was a huge help to me in the bush. He not only carried heavy equipment back and forth, but also contributed to the photographs in my last two books. Hopefully he will continue in my footsteps.

Putting the final product together takes skills and expertise and so thanks to Nicky Wenhold, the talented designer, and Heinrich van den Berg of HPH Publishing for the wonderful end product.

Gerald Hinde

Colossians 3:23

Through my many years of working in the bush and spending time in the wild places of Africa, I have had the privilege of learning from trackers and rangers who are masters in their craft across the continent. They are too many to mention individually, but I thank everyone who has helped me on this journey.

To my friends and colleagues in the travel business, owners of lodges, custodians of the land and others who have afforded me opportunities to take photographs and explore new areas, thank you.

To my beautiful wife Brandy, and my amazing son, Rhys, thanks for being so patient while I have been gone, but also for supporting and accompanying me on many adventures.

To my partner-in-crime, mentor and dear friend Gerald Hinde: who would have thought after more than 20 movies, five books and many, many long lunches, we would still be at it? Thank you, my friend.

Thanks to Heinrich, Nicky and the HPH team for your creativity, professionalism and another outstanding book.

Will Taylor

Copyright © 2022 by HPH Publishing
First Edition
ISBN 978-1-77632-321-0
Text by Will Taylor
Photography by Gerald Hinde
(Rhino beetle on p. 124 by Rassie Jacobs)
Publisher: Heinrich van den Berg
Edited by Diane Mullen
Proofread by Margy Beves-Gibson and
Jane Bowman
Design, typesetting and reproduction by
Heinrich van den Berg and Nicky Wenhold
Printed in China

First edition, first impression 2022
Published by HPH Publishing
50A Sixth Street, Linden, Johannesburg,
2195, South Africa
www.hphpublishing.co.za
info@hphpublishing.co.za

HPH
Publishing